CHANCE THE RAPPER

MUSICIAN AND ACTIVIST

TOM HEAD AND
DEIRDRE HEAD

Enslow Publishing
101 W. 23rd Street
Suite 240
New York, NY 10011
USA

enslow.com

Published in 2020 by Enslow Publishing, LLC.
101 W. 23rd Street, Suite 240, New York, NY 10011

Copyright © 2020 by Enslow Publishing, LLC

All rights reserved.

No part of this book may be reproduced by any means without the written permission of the publisher.

Library of Congress Cataloging-in-Publication Data
Names: Head, Tom, author. | Head, Deirdre, author.
Title: Chance the Rapper : musician and activist / Tom Head and Deirdre Head.
Description: New York : Enslow Publishing, 2020. | Series: Stars of hip-hop | Audience: 2 | Includes bibliographical references and index.
Identifiers: LCCN 2018046991| ISBN 9781978509566 (library bound) | ISBN 9781978510036 (pbk.) | ISBN 9781978510043 (6 pack)
Subjects: LCSH: Chance the Rapper—Juvenile literature. | Rap musicians—United States—Biography—Juvenile literature.
Classification: LCC ML3930.C442 H43 2020 | DDC 782.421649092 [B] —dc23
LC record available at https://lccn.loc.gov/2018046991

Printed in the United States of America

To Our Readers: We have done our best to make sure all websites in this book were active and appropriate when we went to press. However, the author and the publisher have no control over and assume no liability for the material available on those websites or on any websites they may link to. Any comments or suggestions can be sent by email to customerservice@enslow.com.

Photo Credits: Cover, p. 1 Scott Dudelson/Getty Images; p. 5 Jason LaVeris/FilmMagic/Getty Images; p. 7 Jeff Kravitz/Getty Images; p. 8 Kris Connor/Getty Images; p. 11 Matthew Eisman/Getty Images; p. 12 Paul Natkin/Archive Photos/Getty Images; p. 14 Kevin Winter/Getty Images; p. 17 Timothy Hiatt/Getty Images; pp. 18, 25 Daniel Boczarski/Getty Images; p. 20 Barry Brecheisen/Getty Images; p. 23 © AP Images; p. 26 Emma McIntyre/Getty Images.

CONTENTS

1. BECOMING THE RAPPER 4
2. MAKING HISTORY 10
3. CHICAGO'S CHAMPION 16
4. THE FUTURE OF CHANCE 22
   TIMELINE 28
   CHAPTER NOTES 29
   WORDS TO KNOW 31
   LEARN MORE 32
   INDEX 32

BECOMING THE RAPPER

Chance the Rapper's name is Chancelor Bennett. He was born on April 16, 1993, in Chicago. His father, Ken, worked for Barack Obama. His mother, Lisa, worked for the Illinois **attorney general**. Lisa also owned a tobacco farm. Chance has a younger brother named Taylor.

Chance and his brother grew up in Chicago. Chance didn't like rap at first. The first rap album he loved was Kanye West's

debut. It was called *The College Dropout*. It came out when Chance was eleven years old. Chance started rapping. He was talented. Crowds gathered to hear him rap.

RAPPER OR LAWYER?

When Chance was fifteen, Barack Obama became president. Ken brought his sons to meet him. Chance wanted to be a rapper. But Ken had Chance tell the president he

Chance the Rapper attends the 2017 BET Awards.

wanted to be a lawyer. Ken did not think rapping was a good way to make a living. Chance and his father disagreed about his future.

When Chance was seventeen, he was caught smoking pot. His school suspended him for ten days. He spent those days working on his first **mixtape**. He called it *10 Day*. It was named after the suspension. When he went back to school, he kept working on the mixtape.

Instrumentality

Chance's friends called him Chano. He and his friend Jason often rapped together. They called their group Instrumentality. Their song "Good Enough" became popular in Chicago.

Chance the Rapper poses with his parents, Ken and Lisa Bennett, at the 2017 pre-Grammy party.

TALENT AND TRAGEDY

Later that year, Chance went to a house party. He went with his friend Rodney. Rodney was a fellow rapper. They bumped

Chance the Rapper performs at the 2016 Meadows Music and Arts Festival in New York. His dreams of becoming a successful rapper came true.

into a stranger. The stranger stabbed Rodney to death, then ran away. Rodney was one of three friends Chance lost that year. It made him angry and scared.

Chance and his father had a long talk that night. Chance promised to go to college in a year if he didn't become a successful rapper. The next April, his father saw an article in *Forbes* magazine about Chance. It praised his first album. Ken saw that his son was a talented rapper. People liked Chance's work. Ken decided to support Chance's rap career.

"I'm a rapper! You should be able to say that . . . and, like, make someone scared in a good way."[1]

MAKING HISTORY

Chance began 2012 as a young man with big dreams. He was already famous in Chicago. Soon, Chance released *10 Day*. But he didn't sell the mixtape in stores. He gave it away for free online.

Most new rappers make a deal with a record company to sell their music. But Chance was so grateful that people liked his work. He wanted them to have it for free. He calls these releases mixtapes, not albums. Mixtapes are given away for free. Albums cost money.

MAKING HISTORY

Acid Rap

Chance soon became famous. Would he keep putting out free music? He released his second mixtape, *Acid Rap*, in 2013. It was downloaded more than a million times.[1]

BECOMING A SUPERSTAR

Chance's fans in Chicago knew he was talented. *10 Day* showed the world his

Chance visits *Sway in the Morning*, a radio show, on June 19, 2013. He talked about *Acid Rap*.

CHANCE THE RAPPER: MUSICIAN AND ACTIVTIST

talent. He released his third mixtape, *Coloring Book,* in 2016. By this time, Chance was a success. This let him work with many other artists.

Chance performs with his role model, Kanye West, at the 2016 Magnificent Coloring Day Festival in Chicago. Chance put the festival together.

MAKING HISTORY

Chance rapped with Lil Wayne, 2 Chainz, and Future. He recorded a song with Christian gospel singer Kirk Franklin. On *Coloring Book*, Chance showed that he could work with the best. He even got to work with his hero, Kanye West. They did the song "All We Got" together. The song had **vocals** from the Chicago Children's Choir.

"I don't have to carry myself as anybody that I'm not, and people picked up on it."[2]

A NEW KIND OF SUCCESS

Chance made mixtapes popular. Before he became famous, record companies decided who would make it big. Chance put his

Chance makes his thank-you speech at the 59th Grammy Awards after winning for Best Rap Album.

work online for free. This showed other musicians they could do the same thing. Chance even showed that they could make money doing this.

Chance wasn't just successful as a solo artist. His group projects did well, too. He has a band called the Social Experiment. They released a mixtape on iTunes. It was downloaded more than 600,000 times.[3] The mixtape had songs with Janelle Monáe, Erykah Badu, and Busta Rhymes. Chance also rapped on **singles** by Justin Bieber, Big Sean, and John Legend.

CHICAGO'S CHAMPION

Chance grew up in Chicago. So he knew the city's public schools were important. In March 2017, Chance gave one million dollars to the schools. He did this after the governor turned down $215 million for the schools.[1]

But Chance knew this wouldn't be enough. He asked the city's businesses to help **fund** the public schools. He also asked the governor to work with political leaders to solve the school funding problem.

On March 6, 2017, Chance gave one million dollars to the Chicago public schools.

Chance also helped create an organization called SocialWorks. It has raised millions more for Chicago's public schools.

BUSINESS IS GOOD

Chance puts out his music

"I'm not going anywhere. I'm gonna live in Chicago till the day I die." [2]

CHANCE THE RAPPER: MUSICIAN AND ACTIVTIST

online for free. But he still earns a lot of money. Chance began wearing a cap with the number 3 on it. It was to celebrate his third mixtape, *Coloring Book*. It also stands for the **Holy Trinity** in his

Chance wears his famous 3 hat at the opening of the Great Wolf Lodge water park in Illinois in 2018.

Chance's Trademark

In 2014, Chance applied for a **trademark**. It was for the number 3 that's on his products. To use his special 3 logo, companies must pay him some of the money they make.

Christian faith. And it represents his new family: himself, his fiancée Kirsten Corley, and their daughter, Kensli. Kensli was born in September 2015.

Chance gets paid every time something with his number 3 logo is sold. He makes millions from concerts and products. He has also begun an acting career.

CHANCE THE ACTOR

Chance has appeared on the show *Saturday Night Live* a few times. He

CHANCE THE RAPPER: MUSICIAN AND ACTIVTIST

Chance appears with the director of *Slice*, Austin Vesely, at the movie's premiere in Chicago, September 10, 2018.

made a short funny video for the Christmas episode in 2016. He hosted the Thanksgiving episode in 2017. Chance has also gone on *Wild 'n Out*. This is a live rap comedy series on MTV.

Chance also starred in *Slice*. *Slice* is a 2018 funny horror movie about a town where pizza delivery people are being murdered. Chance plays a werewolf detective who delivers pizza. The movie was directed by Austin Vesely. Vesely directed two of Chance's music videos. Like Chance's mixtapes, *Slice* was released online.

THE FUTURE OF CHANCE

For years Chance has called Kensli's mother, Kirsten Corley, his best friend. Chance has given her credit for much of his success. Chance proposed to her at a Fourth of July party in 2018.

Chance wants to be a good father. He wants to be there for Kensli. "[I'm] rapping as if I know she's going to listen," he said. "[Art is] just a reflection. The real

"[Art is] just a reflection. The real thing is my daughter."

Chance and his fiancée, Kirsten Corley, attend a Chicago Bulls vs. New Orleans Pelicans basketball game, on October 8, 2017.

thing is my daughter. I understand what is most important now."[1]

His faith has also played a bigger role in his new work. "I don't make Christian rap," he told *Teen Vogue*, "but I am a Christian rapper."[2]

TOURING THE WORLD

Chance won several Grammy Awards in 2017. Then, he began to tour around the country. This was to **promote** his mixtape *Coloring Book*. He called it the Be Encouraged tour. The tour was successful. Audiences packed every stadium he played. Despite his success, Chance never forgot his family or Chicago. He went home between concerts.

A Special Concert

In July 2018, Chance led a concert for the 50th anniversary of the Special Olympics. The concert raised funds for future Special Olympics projects. Usher, Smokey Robinson, and Jason Mraz also sang.

THE FUTURE OF CHANCE

Chance also began a tour of Asia in 2018. He went to Japan, the Philippines, and Singapore. He has fans all over the world.

Chance was one of several artists celebrating the 50th anniversary of the Special Olympics in 2018.

CHANCE THE RAPPER: MUSICIAN AND ACTIVTIST

Chance (*center*) laughs with his younger brother, Taylor Bennett (*left*), at the 2017 Grammy Awards.

THE FUTURE OF CHANCE

THE NEXT IDEA

The year 2018 was a busy one for Chance. He released four **tracks** as singles. All four singles became popular. He told fans that a fourth mixtape would be released soon.

Chance continues to help Chicago's schools raise money. The principal who suspended Chance is proud of him.

Chance loves his home city of Chicago. He's close to his parents. He's helping his younger brother start his own rap career. Despite this success, Chance has not lost touch with his roots.

TIMELINE

1993 Chance Bennett is born in Chicago on April 16.
2004 Kanye West's debut album, *College Dropout*, is released, igniting young Chance's interest in rap.
2008 Chance begins recording mixtapes with his high school friend Justin (J-Emcee). They perform under the name Instrumentality.
2011 Chance begins writing and recording *10 Day*, his first solo mixtape, during a ten-day suspension from high school.
2012 Chance releases *10 Day* online. This launches his national career.
2013 Chance releases *Acid Rap*.
2014 Chance receives the City of Chicago's annual Outstanding Youth Award.
2015 Along with four other musicians (who collectively call themselves the Social Experiment), Chance the Rapper releases *Surf*.
2015 Chance's daughter, Kensli, is born in September.
2016 Chance releases *Coloring Book*.
2016 Chance wins a BET Image Award for Best New Hip-Hop Artist.
2017 Chance wins Grammy Awards for Best New Artist and Best Rap Performance, as well as an NAACP Image Award for Outstanding New Artist.
2018 Chance becomes engaged to Kirsten Corley.
2018 Chance makes his film debut in the horror comedy *Slice*.

CHAPTER NOTES

CHAPTER 1. BECOMING THE RAPPER

1. Mark Anthony Green, "The Gospel According to Chance the Rapper," *GQ*, February 14, 2017, https://www.gq.com/story/chance-the-rapper-profile-2017.

CHAPTER 2. MAKING HISTORY

1. Billboard Staff, "The Evolution of Chance the Rapper," *Billboard*, October 6, 2016, https://www.billboard.com/articles/columns/hip-hop/7525638/the-evolution-of-chance-the-rapper.

2. Sami Yenigun, "Chance the Rapper on Mixtapes, Politics and Priorities," *The Record*, NPR, August 9, 2017, https://www.npr.org/sections/therecord/2017/08/09/542077601/chance-the-rapper-on-mixtapes-politics-and-priorities.

3. David Renshaw, "Chance the Rapper Reveals Over 600,000 People Have Already Downloaded His Free 'Surf' Album," *NME*, June 6, 2015, https://www.nme.com/news/music/chance-the-rapper-37-1210472.

CHAPTER 3. CHICAGO'S CHAMPION

1. Dakin Andone, "Chance the Rapper Donates $1 Million to Chicago Public Schools," CNN, August 16, 2017, https://www.cnn.com/2017/03/06/us/chance-the-

rapper-donates-1-million-chicago-public-schools/index.html.

2. Resita Cox, "Chance the Rapper on Music, Black Women and His Love for Home: 'I'm Gonna Live in Chicago Till the Day I Die,'" The TRiiBE, March 6, 2018, https://thetriibe.com/2018/03/chance-the-rapper-in-sight-out-pitchfork-mca-chicago/.

CHAPTER 4. THE FUTURE OF CHANCE

1. Brian "Z" Zisook, "How Becoming a Parent Changed Chance's Approach to Making Music," DJBooth, August 9, 2017, https://djbooth.net/features/2017-08-09-chance-the-rapper-parenting.

2. Elaine Welteroth, ed., "Chance the Rapper Opens Up About What It's Like to Challenge Kanye West," *Teen Vogue,* May 16, 2017, https://www.teenvogue.com/story/chance-the-rapper-jordan-peele-cover-interview-music-issue-creativity.

WORDS TO KNOW

attorney general A lawyer who works for the US government or a state government.

debut The first or earliest work.

fund To give money to something.

Holy Trinity An important idea in the Christian faith that God is made up of the Father, the Son (Jesus Christ), and the Holy Spirit.

mixtape A collection of songs recorded by a rapper or a DJ, usually either given away for free or sold at a low cost.

promote To make something known to a wider audience.

single A song release.

track An individual piece of music recorded on an album or mixtape.

trademark A unique symbol that a person or company uses.

vocals Singing parts.

LEARN MORE

BOOKS

Morgan, Joe L. *Hip Hop and R&B: Chance the Rapper.* Broomall, PA: Mason Crest, 2018.

Morse, Eric. *What Is Hip-Hop?* Brooklyn, NY: Akashic Books, 2017.

Niver, Heather Moore. *Chance the Rapper: Hip-Hop Artist.* New York, NY: Enslow Publishing, 2018.

WEBSITES

Chance Raps
chanceraps.com
Visit Chance's official website, featuring his latest music releases and free archived mixtapes.

SocialWorks
socialworkschi.org
Learn more about Chance's nonprofit organization.

INDEX

A
awards, 25

C
charities, 16–17, 24, 27
Chicago public schools, 16–17, 27
Christian faith, 18–19, 23
Corley, Kirsten, 19, 22

D
daughter, 19, 22–23

F
family, 4, 5–6, 9, 27

I
Instrumentality, 6

M
mixtapes, 6, 10, 11, 12–15, 27

S
Social Experiment, 15
SocialWorks, 17

T
3 logo, 18–19

Y
youth, 4–9